TEXAS™

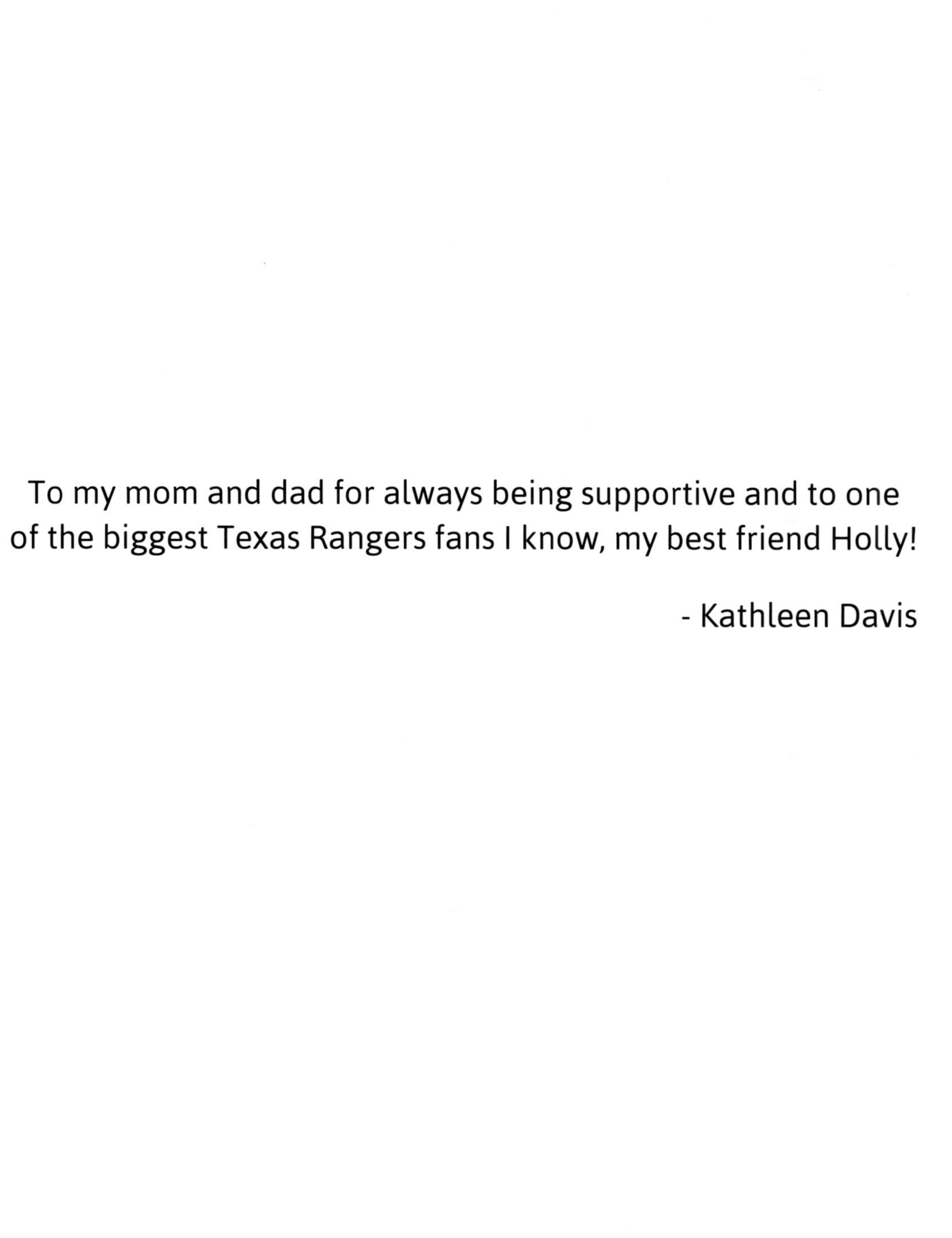

To my mom and dad for always being supportive and to one of the biggest Texas Rangers fans I know, my best friend Holly!

- Kathleen Davis

www.mascotbooks.com

For more information, please contact:
Mascot Books
560 Herndon Parkway #120
Herndon, VA 20170
info@mascotbooks.com

CPSIA Code: PRT1113A
ISBN-10: 1620865688
ISBN-13: 9781620865682

Printed in the United States

It's Baseball Time in Texas!

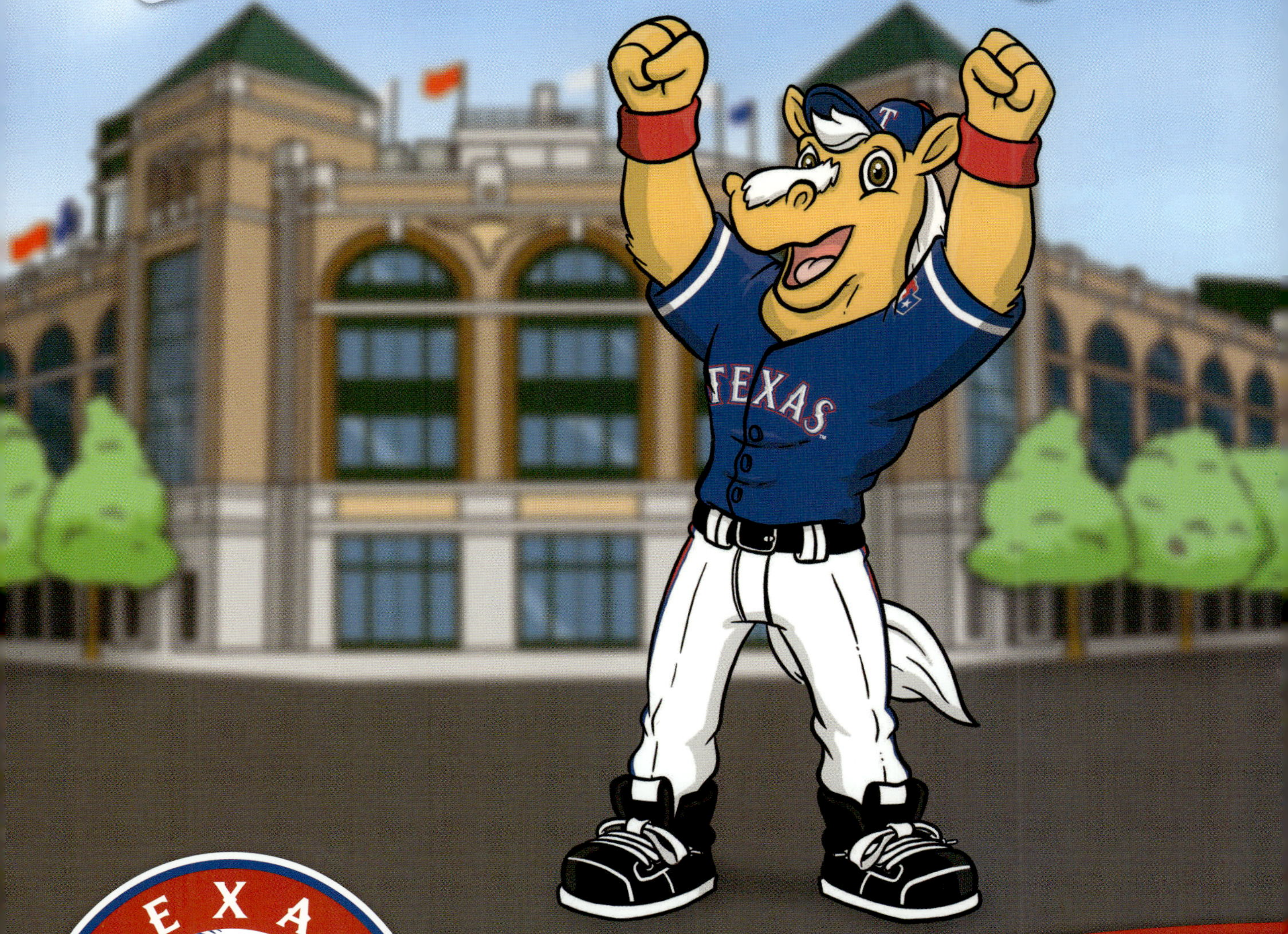

Kathleen Davis
Illustrated by Danny Moore

Rise and shine, *Texas Rangers* fans! It's baseball time in Texas! *Rangers Captain* is at the ballpark ready for the next game.

Rangers Captain spots a family coming to the game. He yells, “Welcome to the ballpark!” and they call back, “Hello, *Rangers Captain*!”

Rangers Captain can't wait to watch his favorite team. It is going to be an exciting day!

Fans cheer, “Let’s go, *Rangers*!” as he rushes into the ballpark.

Rangers Captain is just in time for batting practice. He stands and watches the players get ready for the game.

"It's baseball time in Texas!" says the *Rangers* best hitter as he waves at *Rangers Captain*.

After batting practice, *Rangers Captain* sees the grounds crew proudly preparing the field. He wonders how fast he could run the bases.

As the grounds crew works they holler, “It’s baseball time in Texas!”

Rangers Captain is pretty hungry, so he heads to the concession stands to find some baseball treats! Popcorn, peanuts, cotton candy...what will he eat?

Rangers Captain hears the announcer's big, booming voice and knows he must hurry to the field. He waves at some fans as he runs by and they all cheer, "Let's go, *Rangers*!"

Rangers Captain makes it just in time. He runs onto the field as the players are being introduced.

Rangers Captain cheers, "Let's go, *Rangers*!"
and the crowd roars back!

"PLAY BALL!" yells the umpire, and the game begins.
A fastball is thrown and the batter gets a strike.

Rangers Captain watches closely and cheers, “Let’s go, *Rangers*!”

Rangers Captain walks to visit his fans sitting in their seats.

All the *Rangers* fans are excited to see him and they all cheer,
"Let's go, *Rangers*!"

It's the favorite time of the game for the *Rangers Captain* – the seventh-inning stretch.

Two young *Rangers* fans join him on top of the dugout to sing, "Take Me Out To The Ballgame™".

It’s a quick one, two, three outs and the *Rangers* are up to bat.
The batter takes a swing and it’s going...going...gone!
Right over the center field wall!

Rangers Captain and the players wait for the batter to cross home plate. "*Rangers* win! *Rangers* win!" they all cheer.

What a fun and exciting day! *Rangers Captain* can't wait for it to be baseball time in Texas again.

About the Author

Growing up in the Dallas-Fort Worth area, Kathleen has been a Texas Rangers fan since she was a little girl. Kathleen received her Bachelors degree from Tarleton State University and also received a Masters in Education from Texas Christian University. In her free time, Kathleen enjoys spending time at her family farm in East Texas and, of course, cheering on the Texas Rangers!

MASCOT
BOOKS

TM

TM